This book comes to you as a gift from Scottish Book Trust, as part of Book Week Scotland's celebrations. Over 150,000 of these books will be given away all over Scotland.

Book Week Scotland takes place from 26th November – 2nd December 2012 and is Scotland's first national celebration of books and reading. Throughout the week, libraries, schools, museums, arts venues, charities and workplaces will host a packed programme of events, with ways for people of all ages to celebra͞e ͞ ͞ding. Visit **www.boo** ͞s of Book Week Sc͞ book lists, podcasts ͞e.

D1437710

Scottish Book Trust is the leading agency for the promotion of literature, reading and writing in Scotland, developing innovative projects to encourage adults and children to read, write and be inspired by books. For more information on Scottish Book Trust's projects go to **www.scottishbooktrust.com**.

First published 2012
by Scottish Book Trust

Broadcast by BBC Radio Scotland

Printed and bound by CPI Books
Typeset in 9.5pt Helvetica Neue Light by Stewart Bremner
Cover design by Size Graphic Design

Contents

ARTWORKS ON THE THEME

SCOTLAND'S FAVOURITE PLACES

The Friendly Falls

Michael Palin

I T'S HARD TO know where to begin. Scotland is so richly endowed with great landscapes, breathtaking views and fine cities that picking out a favourite place seems unfair to all the others. But if I had to narrow my focus and forget the Forth–Clyde canal walk in Glasgow, the Bruichladdich Distillery on Islay and the King's House Hotel in Glencoe, I'd settle for the Falls of Dochart in Killin. They're dramatic without being fierce and the way the water twists and tumbles over the rocks is pleasing rather than awesome. They're accessible too. You can get close to them. Thrilling for a child, I should think, and not intimidating to an oldie like me. I'd call them the friendly falls. So much of what is beautiful about Scotland has water at the heart of it, whether it's the rivers and streams, or the lochs and sounds and firths into which they flow. One of the great delights of a visit to the Falls of Dochart is their location. From whichever direction you approach the landscape is magnificent. From the west the valley of the Dochart leads you towards the Falls, with Ben More the sentinel to the south, rising over 1100 metres. Coming at them from the east the road runs, for fourteen glorious miles, beside the silver finger of Loch Tay with the dark flanks of the Ben Lawers range rising over 1200 metres on the far side. Powerful, mysterious, hugely impressive highland scenery.

I think though that a favourite place has to be something more than just an aesthetic choice. There have to be personal elements. And so there are with me and the

Falls of Dochart. In my mid-teens I'd met a girl on holiday in Suffolk, and we'd got on very well. The next year we'd met up again by the chilly grey North Sea and our holiday romance blossomed again. The year after that she wasn't there and I was, for a while, very sad, as I never expected to see her again. Two years later, through the letterbox, came one of those significant communications that can change the course of a lifetime, like unexpectedly good exam results or a successful job application. In my case it was a postcard with a picture of the Falls of Dochart on the front. On the back was a message from the girl I'd never expected to see again. She was on holiday up in the Highlands and had heard via a friend that I had got into Oxford University. This was followed by some snide reference to the fact that they must have lowered their standards, which, as humour had always been at the heart of our relationship, I found deeply reassuring. Reunited by the Falls of Dochart, we later met up and the holiday romance has since developed into a forty-six year marriage.

Was it predestination or just plain good fortune that led me to another relationship that was to shape my life, and which was to bring me to see the Falls of Dochart for myself? Whilst at Oxford I met and started to write with a Welshman from Esher in Surrey called Terry Jones. A few years later, by way of the *Frost Report* and *Do Not Adjust Your Set*, he and I teamed up with three fellow writers and performers from Cambridge, called Idle, Cleese and Chapman. Joined by an American animator named Gilliam, we became Monty Python's Flying Circus. After a few years of television we wrote and produced our first film, *Monty Python and The Holy Grail*. Among many other things it featured a killer rabbit that lived in the terrifying Cave of Caerbannog. The film was almost entirely shot in Scotland and the home of the killer rabbit was on the hillside overlooking Loch Tay. Which is how, on May 6th 1974, on an afternoon free of filming, I first saw the Falls of Dochart for myself. I was with John Cleese and we sat on the rocks with the water spilling around us and talked about the future of Python and John's urge to be free of his obligations to the group. When the time came to go, my hired car wouldn't start and John helped me push it up the hill to Killin's only garage.

In 2005, Terry Jones and myself returned to Scotland to film a short video of our search for the Holy Grail locations which was to be included in a new DVD release. By now, just over thirty years after John had expressed his frustrations with the group, the Holy Grail had been a huge international success and transformed the outlook for Python. We had stayed together, on and off, for two more films, *Life of Brian* and *The Meaning of Life*.

Before Terry and I went on our quest to rediscover the location of the Cave of Caerbannog I insisted that we stop at the Falls. I stepped carefully out onto a rock in the middle of the river, sat down, took my shoes off and dangled my feet in the cool fast-flowing waters of the Dochart. I thought about my life and how this place had come to mean so much to me.

Seven years have gone by since then. John Cleese has just got married, for the fourth time, Terry Jones and I are meeting for a drink tomorrow and my wife has just rung to check on our three-year-old grandson who has come down with what he calls chicken pops. And a few hundred miles north the river will be bubbling and swirling down the Falls of Dochart. ■

Favourite Place

Liz Lochhead

We would be snaking up Loch Lomond, the
road narrow and winding after the turn at Tarbert,
and we'd be bending branches as we slid
through the green and dripping overhang of the trees.
All the bickering over the packing, and the – as usual –
much, much later-than-we'd-meant-to leaving,
all that falling from us,
our moods lifting, lightening, becoming our good mood
the more miles we put
between our freed and weekend selves and Glasgow.

Driving in the dark means: slot in another CD
without even looking at what it is,
another any-old-silver-disc from the zippered case
that, when you reminded me, I'd have quickly stuffed
far too full and randomly, then jammed it,
last minute, into the top of my rucksack.
Golden oldies, yours or mine, whose favourite?
Anyway, the music would spool us through Tyndrum,
past the shut Real Food Cafe where other days
    we like to stop,
and over moonscape Rannoch Moor to the
moonlit majesty of Glencoe,
over the bridge at Ballachulish, past Corran
with the ferry stilled and the loch like glass;
we'd be wriggling along Loch Linnhe then
    straighten up
past the long strip of darkened lochside Big Hotels
    and their

Vacancies or No Vacancies signs
to 30 mph Fort William –
Full-Of-Rain-Town-With-Its-Limitless-Litres-In-A-Mist! –
we'd shout it out and we'd be honouring a
long ago and someone else's family pass-the-time-car-
        journey game we never even played, but Michael,
proud of his teenage wordsmith son,
once told us about – and it has stuck.
We'd be speeding up now, taking the bend's wide
        sweep as
we bypass the sleeping town, making for
the second-last turn-off: Mallaig and The Road
        To The Isles.
And you'd say,
'Last thirty miles, Lizzie, we'll be there by midnight.'

The always longest fifteen miles from Glenfinnan
        to Lochailort
and a wee cheer at the last turn,
down past the big house and the fish farm,
beyond the lay-by – full of travellers' ramshackle vans
now the yellow's on the broom again –
our eyes peeled now for the white-painted stone
        so we'll not miss
the overgrown entrance to the field of caravans.

There would be that sigh of
always glad-to-see our old van still standing,
opening the door, the sniffing – no dampness,
        no mice...
I'd be unloading the first cool bags of food,
while you'd be round the van's side, down in the mud
turning the stopcock for the water,

fixing the gas – and soon,
breathing a big sigh, laughing in relief at
how that huge stag that had suddenly filled the
 windscreen a mile back
stopping our hearts as – ho! – we'd shouted our alarm
had somehow astonishingly leapt free, was gone,
and no harm done,
we'd be lighting candles, pouring a dram,
drinking the first cup of tea
from the old black and white teapot.

And tonight the sky would be huge with stars.
Tomorrow there would be the distant islands
cut out of sugar paper, or else cloud, the rain
 in great veils
coming in across the water, the earliest tenderest
feathering of green on the trees, mibbe autumn
laying bare the birches stark white.
There would be blood-red rowan berries,
 that bold robin
eating from my plate again, or – for a week or two
 in May –
the elusive, insistent cuckoo,
or else the slow untidy flapping of the flight
 of the heron,
the oil-black cormorant's disappear-and-dive,
shifts of sun, double or even treble rainbows.
The waterfall would be a wide white plume or a
thin silver trickle, depending...
There would be bracken's early unfurling or
late summer's heather pinking and purpling over,
 there'd be

a plague of hairy caterpillars and the last
        drunken bees.
Mibbe you'd nudge me, and, hushed,
again we'd watch that otter swim to shore
on New Year's Day with a big fish in its mouth, emerge
so near us on the flat rocks we
wouldn't dare to breathe as we'd watch it,
unconcerned, oblivious,
make a meal of eating it before our eyes.
Or it would be a late Easter this year and,
everywhere along the roadside,
the chrome-yellow straight-out-of-the-tube-and-
laid-on-with-a palette-knife brashness, the
amazing coconut smell of the gorse.

But tonight you are three months dead
and I must pull down the bed and lie in it alone.
Tomorrow, and every day in this place
these words of Sorley MacLean's will echo
        through me:
The world is still beautiful, though you are not in it.
And this will not be a consolation
but a further desolation.

∎

Black Cuddy

James Robertson

'BLACK CUDDY!' Black Cuddy liftit his heid when he heard the lassie cryin him, syne he wis aff, canterin ower the laich park tae whaur she wis waitin. She had a puckle carrots for him in her pooch, sweet as caramel, and she fed him three but kept yin back for efter. He let her clap his neck and his neb, and he pit his hot braith tae her lug and peched.

'Whit are ye sayin the day, Black Cuddy?' she spiered. He sometimes tellt her secrets when she cam tae see him. But Black Cuddy didna say onythin. He shook his muckle heid at her. Awa up the brae tae the widds, and see whit the cushie-doos are sayin. Sae she clapped him yince mair for luck, and awa up the brae she gaed.

The day wis fine and the widds looked as braw as ever she'd seen them. Chaffies were cheetlin and a widdpecker chappin, the gress tummocks were saft and the maisies shone like wee suns amang the roots o the trees. At the tap o the brae, in a big auld birk, twa doos were newsin. 'Whit are ye sayin, cushie-doos?' she spiered. Och, this and thon. Awa tae the burn and see whit the watter-craw's sayin.

The watter-craw wis dookin in wee pools o the burn, lookin for her denner as the watter gaed chirlin and kecklin ower the chuckies. 'Whit are ye sayin, wee bird?' she spiered. I'm ower thrang, I'm ower thrang. Awa tae the loch and see whit the heron is sayin.

Lang Sandy wis up tae his knees in the loch. He wis still as a stookie. The loch wis a skimmerin brooch, and the hills aw aboot were a plaid, green and gowden, russet and reid, broon and blae. She stood and she stared, but afore she could spier it wis Wheesht! Can ye no see I'm fushin? Awa tae the reeds and see whit the puddocks are sayin.

The puddocks were haudin some kind o convention. They stopped when they heard her steps on the grund. 'Whit are ye on aboot, puddocks?' she spiered. But they aw took the dorts, like she'd fund them oot tellin a lee. Nuthin, we didna say nuthin. Awa tae the bank and see whit the troot is sayin.

But the troot wis asleep in a haud o the bank. She widna come up tae the licht. The lassie lay doon and dippit her haun and guddled, but the troot didna shift. The flees bizzed aboot. We're no feart, we're no feart, no fae her, no fae you. Awa tae the cleg and see whit he's sayin.

But the lass didna gang tae the cleg. The cleg cam tae her. He landit licht as a gliff on her airm. At first she didna jist ken he wis there. Syne she did. 'Och, cleg, dinna bite. Dae whit ye like, but please dinna bite.'

Whit are ye sayin, dinna bite, dinna bite? I'm a cleg, that's ma joab. Whit'll ye gie me tae mak me no bite?

'I'll gie ye a secret that naebody kens.'

Oh aye? Whit's that? And wha disna ken it?

'Awbody. Black Cuddy didna tell me, sae he disna ken. The cushie-doos dinna ken. The watter-craw wisna sayin. Lang Sandy wisna sayin. The puddocks' mooths were steekit. The troot wis in a dwam. The flees were jist glaikit. But I ken fine.'

Tell me then, whit is this secret?

'Dae ye sweir no tae bite?'

Weel... aye, aw richt.

'This,' said the lassie, lookin aboot her, 'is the bonniest, brawest place in the warld. And naebody kens it but me, and yersel.'

Is that it? And the cleg bit her hard, and sooked at her blood.

'Aiya!' she yelped. 'Ye said ye widna,' she grat. She skelped at her airm, but the cleg wis awa. That'll learn ye, cam floatin back on the breeze.

By, but her airm wis sair. She gaed tae the lochside and cooled it wi watter. That'll learn ye. Whit wid it learn her? The flees bizzed aboot. They didna ken. Whit a sin, whit a sin! We widna dae thon. The troot woke and rose, and gawped at the lassie, and swallied a flee. The lassie walked on.

The puddocks were pappin and plowtin like parritch. Oh man, oh man, that's some bite that. Ye should get that seen tae. Crabbit auld cleg. At least they made her laugh wi their daft cairry-on.

Lang Sandy fleed by wi a fush in his mooth. Canna stop noo, I'm gaun hame for ma tea.

Doon at the burnside she sat for a while. The cauld watter soothered her airm and wis sweet in her thrapple. The watter-craw watched frae the tap o a stane. Ach, ye'll no dee o it, hen. And she kent that she widna. But it didna stop it bein sair.

The doos were aye in their tree, yatterin on. Och noo, och noo. Puir sowl, puir sowl.

'I'm fine, thanks,' she said, gaun doon through the widds. But she kent they werena really speakin tae her.

When she wis back at the dyke she cried Black Cuddy, and he cam tae her, jist as he aye did. She gied him the last carrot, and clapped his neck, and he pit his hot braith tae her lug and peched.

Whit did the cushie-doos say?

She shook her heid.

Whit did the water-craw say?

She shook her heid again.

Whit did the heron say?

Whit did the puddocks say?

Whit did the troot say?

Whit did the flees say?

Whit did the cleg say?

'He tellt me a lee and he gied me a bite.'

Whit for did he gie ye a bite?

'I tellt him a secret and he didna much like it.'

And whit wis the secret?

'That this is the bonniest, brawest place in the warld.'

But we aw ken that. Whit for did he bite ye?

The lassie showed him the yellae lump on her airm.

'Tae learn me.'

Tae learn ye?

'Sae I widna forget,' she said. ∎

The Wall Song

Aidan Moffat

There's a picture of you on that wall
as the sun sets down on the town hall,
with a hopeful smile but head held down,
watching buses breaking out of town.

We had to make some big decisions
so we gossiped till the sun was gone;
soon you'd be studying at uni,
and soon I'd be signing on.

And the cells where we will spend the night
when they misconstrue a friendly fight
after getting drunk with secret skill,
just a moment from us up the hill.

How many nights did we run by here
with the Casuals on our heels?
How much cheap wine was swigged and swallowed
as we dined on deep-fried meals?

They swung their skates and spat
but at least they missed your head,
and I heard a rumour that
at least one of them's now dead.
But the buses stopped for us
after a few more idle years,
and we fled without much fuss,
in search of cradles and careers.

It's a picture of you I can't find,
but forever mounted in my mind;
of the place where we would dream and vow,
and I wonder where you might be now.

■

To hear Aidan Moffat singing this song and to download it for free, please visit www.scottishbooktrust.com/myfavouriteplace/ celebrities/aidan-moffat.

An t-àit' as àille

Aonghas Phàdraig Caimbeul

Aon latha
coltach ri gach latha eile,
phut m' athair mi
suas an cnoc air a' bhaidhseagal,
mar bu dual.
Aon làmh mhòr a' stiuireadh na dìollaid,
an tè eile air a'chrann. Thionndaich sinn,
a' coimhead sìos a' bhràigh, 's ruith e,
gach làmh a-nis air an dìollaid
's tughadh taigh Bean Liondsaidh a' seòladh seachad
's an ath rud cha chluinninn brag a bhrògan
leis a' ghaoith a' sèideadh trom cheann
's mi 'g itealaich deas, saor,
le sùil bheag gum chùl far an robh esan
mìltean is mìltean air ais
aig mullach a' chnuic,
a' smèideadh.

∎

My Favourite Place

Angus Peter Campbell

One day
no different from any other day,
my father pushed me
up the hill on the bike,
as usual.
One enormous hand guiding the saddle,
the other balancing the handlebar. We turned,
looking down the brae, and he began to run,
both hands now on the saddle
as Bean Liondsaidh's thatched house flew by
and the next thing I couldn't hear
his feet for the wind rushing through my head
as I flew south, freewheeling,
glancing back to see him
miles and miles away
at the top of the hill,
waving.

■

Of Mice and Haggises

Sally Magnusson

THERE IS A particular quality of evening light in early summer, just before the day turns. Every line you see – the branch of a tree, the curve of a distant hill – is sharpened in it. The green of the fields is emerald-bright and the blue of the sky (of this you are sure) is the acme of all blues there ever were. You walk along, spirits soaring with the joy of it. Suddenly everything makes sense. And then, by infinitesimal degrees, the light begins to fade, the lines start to blur and smudge, the grass confesses to a hint of brown and someone has taken a rubber to the sky. That time of utter clarity, that ecstatic Wordsworthian moment of seeing into the life of things, is no more. You call the dog and remember the ironing is waiting.

Yes, it can take the imagination to wonderful places, this haunt of mine, although it is nothing grand in itself: just a walk in farming countryside north of Glasgow. I follow a tumbling burn along a tree-strewn bank, climb a steep track to a point below the Campsie Hills where I can catch my breath and gaze at the city spread out below, then head down again. The dog and I amble there and back most days and I wish I could claim such poetic uplift every time. In fact I am usually listening to a podcast of *The Archers*, and in the whole of the recorded universe there is nowhere more prosaic than Ambridge. But, oh, I love this place. I love the golden light of those May evenings. I love the daffodil fiesta in March. I adore the wild flowers that tangle the verges in July. I even relish plodding along in the dreich drizzle of a January afternoon when the trees drip and the snowdrops cower and the light never has the chance of an artistic death because it has barely lived in the first place.

Best of all I love knowing this place so well that I can slip into its moods and seasons like a slipper. I know where the ice will trip me in winter and where the wild garlic will send out its pungent whiff of early summer. I know where the primroses hide and where tiny raspberries will flaunt their sweetness behind an armour of nettles. I know the smell, the lovely smell, of the rain-sodden earth.

On the other hand, beloved places can be like beloved people: you know them, and you don't know them. Today I experienced a familiar thrill at the sight of frost lacing the old drystane dyke. But minutes later I discovered something quite new – to me at least. I noticed how many of the tree-trunks and branches that I previously thought were quite bare are in fact exquisitely embroidered with ice-green lichen. I crumbled off a piece and marvelled at this unremarked colony of tiny leaf-like shapes. Why had I never noticed before?

And then there are the memories. This place is all about remembering.

The daffodils shooting up again as I write in February are the ones the children and I planted together one balmy afternoon long ago. The burn is where they built dams and rescued misdirected footballs. These desiccated bramble bushes prompted our first and last attempt to make jam one autumn. The toads we swerve to avoid in the mating season used to be collected by a soft-hearted son, who hopped out of the car and tenderly moved each one to the side of the road; in those days a frog could have crawled home faster than we did on a rainy night.

The hill is the scene of family egg-rolling competitions on Easter Day, so hotly contested that last year another son rigged up a pulley between telegraph poles to carry his egg to the finish line. (The year before he attached it to a firework and the year before that prodded the dog to carry it around her neck. His efforts always end in disaster.)

That gaunt hawthorn tree, waiting and waiting for the cloud of creamy blossom that will transform it in late spring, is the one my mother loved. Walking past it together, we used to dip our heads into the flowery froth and wonder at the strange absence of fragrance.

When the wild flowers arrive, they remind me of the summer I once devoted to learning their names: tufted vetch and self-heal, slender speedwell and meadowsweet, hoary cinquefoil, thyme-leaved sandwort, yellow loose-strife, sneezewort, buttercup, foxglove, forget-me-not. Weeds? They are flowers as beguiling as their names.

The birds are old friends, too: the owl with its unearthly night-call, the huge buzzard soaring overhead, the circling hawk, the heron that pays a hopeful visit to the burn and then stands there looking silly, the interminably squawking crows. Then there is the family of deer that skitter out of the way as soon as the dog heralds our approach, a fox or two, a scurry of tiny rabbits, a dashing field-mouse, even the occasional otter in the pool under the bridge.

One spring day, when the gorse had burst canary-yellow across the hillside and the trees were budding along the bank, it occurred to me that this place would make a perfect setting for a children's book populated by these same animals and birds. By the end of the week I had the plot of *Horace the Haggis*, the story of a lone haggis on the run who finds refuge here with a blethery mouse, a vegetarian fox, a pair of tweeting magpies, a gossiping rook, an inventor squirrel and the bumbling underground intelligence agency, the Mole Patrol. I dare say that before publication later this year I will have to explain to the gentle farmer at the top of the hill why, in the interests of art, he has been reborn as a wicked haggis-hunter in underpants decorated with tulips.

That, of course, is the thing about a favourite place. You just never know where it will transport you next. ■

Favourite Place

Alexander McCall Smith

MY FAVOURITE place is a watery place, the top end of the Sound of Mull. The sound begins where Morvern turns a corner into Loch Linnhe. To the south of that point is Lismore, and beyond that Oban and the islands that cluster about it. That is the route to Jura and Islay, but we are looking north now, making our way past Lochaline and the ruins of Ardtornish Castle, up past Fiunary, to Drimnin on the Morvern shores and Tobermory on the Mull side. Now we are in the patch of water that I love to cross in my gaff-rigged cutter, either under sail or with the diesel engine thumping away down below. More often it is with the engine on, as the winds here can be eccentric and unreliable, funnelled or blocked by various mountains that have little sympathy for the needs of the sailor.

It is a place of blues and silvers, and occasional golds. The sea has many moods: at times it may be flat calm, and milky, untroubled by even the slightest breeze. In such conditions, the surface will speak to what lies below: sudden stirrings will occur as shoals of tiny fish seek to escape voracious mackerel, attracting the attention of mewing gulls or diving birds, or there may be the slick black shape of a porpoise, darting, cavorting, cutting through the water like a small torpedo. At other times, especially when the tide draining down the sound meets a strong wind blowing the other way, it is a place of turbulence and liquid excitement. White horses top steel-grey waves, and as the wind picks up, foam may be whipped across the surface of the sea.

Up at the top end of the sound, from a point to the west of the rocks known as the Stirks, you can look up towards Ardnamurchan Head or across the stretch of water that lies between the mainland and the islands, and see, on the horizon, the smudge of land that is Coll. In a reasonably fast boat, the time taken to make the crossing is a couple of hours at the most. Once there, you can anchor around the Cairns of Coll and step off on to a beach of brilliant white. At the edge of the beaches there is that mixture of grass and flowers that is common on those lovely islands: purple and yellow flowers dot the grass on which here and there one finds a fragment of white shell, a tuft of wool from a blackface sheep, a feather from a seabird, some bleached sticks thrown up by the waves.

In good weather, once you have turned the corner round Ardnamurchan Head, you look up to Muck, to Rum, to Eigg, with Skye behind them, and Moidart reaching up to the sky to the north-east. I look back at Mull, and remember the lines of the poet, Ruthven Todd, who stacked peat on the island during a summer in the 1930s and who wrote about the hills crouching like lions against the Atlantic. These hills, this sea, these islands against the Atlantic, the various shades of blue, fill the heart with feeling. I am happy here. I am happy that this place is as it is. I do not want to be anywhere else. ■

Scotland's Favourite Places:

The following pieces were selected from over 800 submissions made to the My Favourite Place project in 2012. They are all by members of the public.

G is for Glasgow

Aileen Jardine

Gallus, gritty, golden, gruesome
gigantic green-spaces and grubby (back)greens
greetin'-faced googooers and gin-sodden grannies
glad-eyed goolie-grabbers and gullible gals
gentleman gangsters and gash-faced gang-members
geared-up ganja-smokers and giant-hearted gift givers
garlic-breathed gluttonists and groovy gig-goers
Green goalscorers and Ger's goalies (or vice versa)
G12-dwellers and Govanites
Garngad grandfaithers and Garrowhill glamourpusses
gap-toothed geezers and gossipy gasbags
ginger-heided gits and ginger-heided goddesses
glass-eyed gogglebox-watchers and gabby gobshites
golden gents, good girls, glorious grandparents
grateful Glaswegians, guid glorious Glesga.

gonnae no do that gonnae no
games-a-bogey
∎

An Invitation

Lynn Blair

THERE'S A particular pitch within your just-awake brain, a cadence of sleepy openness that's useful if you want to write, and it's easily chased away. So excuse me if I don't put the lights on. We'll have to bumble in the dark, light a candle while I boil the kettle for tea and fill a hot water bottle. It's winter. Life can only happen from within these little puddles of heat. I'll pull on last night's jumper over my pyjamas. If I were to get dressed properly now I'd have to consider the day ahead, begin listing the possibilities. Okay! Tea, laptop, mighty Arctic jumper. Ready?

We're not going far. The back-door lock is trouble-some to negotiate with one free hand, but then you get the hit of freezing air rushing into your lungs, an icy kiss on your cheeks as we cross the back garden. There's usually a whisper of the cats and foxes that have just exited stage left, maybe a sliver of moon, reassuringly sturdy in a purpling sky. The street is soundless. Behind us, in deepest slumber, four children occupy two rooms, my husband a third.

It's an unusual shape this shed, five-sided and the only one we could find to squeeze into this corner of the garden. I've lost the tiny key so often that I've attached it to a child's trainer. The day before we built it I handed my family black pens and they wrote merry words on the foundation slabs. Next day the walls went up – twice – the midges nibbled and the neighbours twitched. Beer was consumed. When the roof was on and the windows in, I painted it the softest yellow, the colour you get when you cream together butter and sugar for a cake. It felt like mine then.

Please, come in, make yourself at home. We're rocking the austerity vibe at the moment. There's some leftover grey carpet on the floor, a purple desk to write at (chipboard, four sticks of equal length and masonry paint), a bookshelf with my heart's desires and an old gas fire. I'm pretty sure it's not a health risk, but I'll get it spluttering anyway – it's preferable to hypothermia. Please ignore the A3 paper on the walls covered in sub-divisions of my imagination and wonder instead at the weird collection of postcards and ripped out bits of magazines. Funny what you'll admit inspires you when no one else is looking. You can have the sun-lounger. Yes, I know I'm supposed to be busy, but I have four children and even the strongest coffee doesn't always pierce the pea-souper created by two-year-old twins. Naps do.

Come evening we can pull the blinds down, light all the candles and put on the fairy lights. Pour a glass of wine and draw a picture or two. Make notes on the blackboard on the back of the door. Study the faces I've collected on cork boards and try to figure out how they'll stitch into whatever story I'm knitting. There's a radio for music, or that weird comfort of faraway voices, but no electricity so you need to be organised – charge up the laptop, power the twinkly lights with batteries. But you can work here in silence. Or dream.

That tree right outside the window was barely more than a twig when my dad gave it to me, years ago. I nearly killed it as it sat neglected outside the con-verted garage I called home when I was a student. Four years later I married, moved to a cottage and painted the walls in rainbow colours. The tree, still in the same cracked pot, was plonked on the doorstep and ignored. It endured somehow. Circumstances brought us here, to a town full of roundabouts where we made a family and conjured a garden. I planted my neglected stick without much hope, yet nonetheless offered spells of encouragement to its crushed roots. Of course all it needed was this space I'd finally offered it. Some room of one's own to spread roots and grow leaves. It now has wind chimes hanging from the branches and birds queuing up at the feeders. It battles with the prevailing wind, as I play with words, two late starters relishing the patch of this earth that finally allows us to explore as we should.

The sun will come up soon, my children will wake and I'll go and pour juice and wipe spilled Weetabix. That's my love, my adored life. But the existence of this place is an expression of intent. When I'm struggling I can no longer hide my laptop under the newspapers and pretend I'll get round to it one day. This little yellow shed summons me and invites me to persevere. This place – the one that I created – allows me to own my life unequivocally.

I'm not alone. I glimpse these pods of magic all over Scotland: the urban balcony overflowing with salad and flowers; the tumbledown porch, where an easel and some vivid looking jam jars teem with paint; the bedroom table where the sewing stuff is a permanent fixture. There's a walk-in cupboard uprising going on, an unused corner reformation. Imagine, if you will, a future in a country full of people thoroughly nourished and emboldened by their inventiveness. These small spaces aren't commercial – and are precious enough for that reason alone – but they have prodigious returns paid in spirit.

So I propose an alternative sort of Doors Open Day, one where, like this one, the guide apologises for the pile of muddy shoes in the hallway, then leads you to a slightly wonky shed and feeds you cake. You might, quite correctly, mention the problems you'll encounter in making time, making space in your life. And I'd speak of your one precious life and the giddy treasure of wrenched-out hours in a tiny space where the possibilities are boundless.

Come and visit anytime. ∎

Traigh a' Mhill
56°16'40"N 6°19'50"W
West Looking East /
East Looking West

David Faithfull

56°16'40"N/6°19'50"W : 05 MAP 48/NM 1313T
PEATY GLEYS + RANKERS, BLANKET + FLYING BENT B.
ATLANTIC + BOREAL HEATHER MOOR, ROSS OF MULL GR⎯
ROCKY + RUGGED SLOPES : 414 MILLION YEARS OLD

TRAIGH A'MHILL: BÀH OF THE LUMP/OGRES.
THE BÀH OF THE BEES, HONEY BEES BUSY ON
THE LOWER SLOPES AS CAREFULLY WE GO
BAREFOOT ON THE SWEET HONEY COLOURED S...

On Harris (Nymphaea Alba)

Donald Urquhart

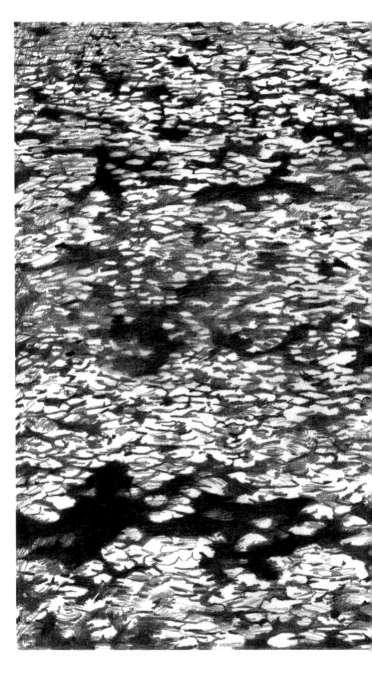

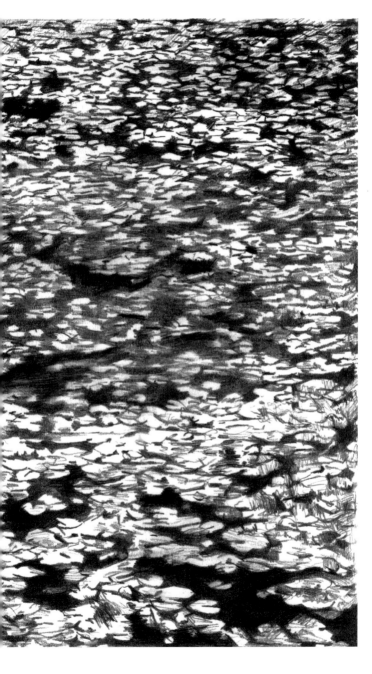

Women Around the World (Glasgow Women's Library)

Kate Davis

Rannoch Sunset

Peter Ewing

SOLITUDE IS a relative term. Nowhere in Scotland is more than six miles from a metalled road. But six miles of solitude is still worth seeking out.

The Scottish environmentalist John Muir once said 'Break clear away, once in a while, and climb a mountain, or spend a week in the woods. Wash your spirit clean.' This trip was going to be a power shower rather than a long soak in the tub.

The long road to Rannoch Station is technically a dead end, but to my mind, a vibrantly alive one. I parked at the station and unlashed the canoe from the roof bars. It took a while because it was tied down with Mason knots – named after the Canadian paddler who observed: 'I only know one knot. But when it really matters, I tie a lot of them.'

A light breeze had driven the midges away. My mobile phone didn't work – excellent – but there was a phone box like a scarlet monolith in the moorland. I phoned my wife to let her know I was setting off. It was a very short call. Every midge on Rannoch Moor was sheltering from the breeze in that phone box.

'Portage' is one of those words that makes middle-aged men feel like Hawkeye the Pathfinder, but after half a mile I was very glad to get the canoe off my shoulders and into its proper environment of Loch Laidon. The breeze had dropped and the water was like quicksilver. Paddling a windless loch is more like flying – the sky is both above and below you. Around me was the vastness of Rannoch Moor.

It's a strange place. It was once a wilderness of Scots pines, with bear and lynx padding the needled floor. Now it is peat and heather, a few patches of commercial forestry, red deer and buzzards. Yet the past is still present, because the peat is riddled with skeletal tree roots, the colour of ivory. This is the ossuary of a long-dead forest. Like the iron harvest of the Flanders farmer, the past won't stay buried.

I incised the water with another dip of maple paddle and glided south-west down the loch. I'd left my watch behind, so I looked at the western sky.

The horizon was black and gold, but not for long. The sun was flowing behind the mountains like sand in an hourglass, fast enough for the movement to be visible. It struck me that our sun must always cross the sky with such speed, but without a reference point we fail to notice it. Time can be like that too.

There were two islands in the loch – tiny forests arising from a watery looking glass that stretched away, beyond the bow, further than I could see. I considered the more distant island, but the wise outdoorsman does not choose to make camp in the dark. I glanced at the map. The island did not have a name. Antarctica and Alaska must surely have nameless places, but I felt a curious delight that Scotland had them too.

I beached the canoe on the shore, the jagged schist putting another scar in the hull. The island was a refugee of the Caledonian wildwood – preserved by its moat. Pine and birch, needle and leaf, rock and water. It was a forest in miniature, a relic, a time machine. Wilderness, if you like.

I rigged my hammock between a pair of trees, brewed a pail of tea, and listened to the silence, and the gentle hum of my spirit on the deep-clean cycle. ∎

Kellie Road

Hannah Lavery

THE SCHOOL rush is soundtracked by our squawking and screeching. As the minutes move perilously close to the last one, we become a thunderous cloud, speeding out of the house.

We move, with much noise, down and out of our street. My hair is unbrushed and I try to tame it by tucking it behind my ears. My boy is moving slowly on his scooter; his foot, in his new school shoes, drags and scrapes against the pavement. The toddler and the baby, still covered in their breakfast, are strapped in, and screaming in their double buggy. There is so much to forget and it is not until we reach Kellie Road that I allow myself a slow breath. I release my boy from all my nagging and let him speed off to join the others.

The road is bustling with the children in uniform, with the mummies, and daddies, the childminders, grannies, and grandas. Dressed in overalls, and in suits, for the gym, for housework, and for a quick coffee. We are pushing buggies, holding little hands, walking the dog, on bikes. Bikes, pulling trailers of babies, attached to tag-alongs, riding slowly behind and in front like the sergeant major or the mother hen. Wee ones slow on their first bikes, in awe of the older ones whooshing past. The young girls impressively rock their hips on their wiggle boards and groups of friends move as a herd or a gaggle, and we all move down the long road, chatting, catching up, complaining, arranging. We holler to slow our children down.

I move aside for a hanging branch, and I look away from the rush into the quiet of the woods. The old trees, and newly planted ones, the sways of flowers, nettles and grasses. Today, there is a wee lost shoe hanging on the branch; the rooks are cawing out. I imagine their calls are for the child without a shoe. The bright blue shoe sitting like a jewel on the dark green. My toddler shouts out, 'Booshoo!', and I say, 'Yes, booshoo'.

He points into the trees as a squirrel runs up a thick trunk. I stop and bend down beside him, and we point together, but soon lose the squirrel as it leaps to a higher branch, and then to a faraway tree. My 'ready for school' boy is waiting up ahead, and he shouts at us to hurry up.

A mass of scooters parts to avoid a big fat juicy slug. Its naked fat body, its deep thick lines, its glossy head, its size and markings makes me think of a baby hedgehog. I think then about the quiet little hedgehog we saw in the path a few months past. I wonder do they remember him too. My baby is now crying; I stop and put on the sling and gather her up out of the buggy. I strap her close. We walk on a little faster to catch my boy up.

He has stopped now, and with his friends, he is reaching into the wood to pick the raspberries. He smiles at me as he pops one in his mouth, and he is off down the road again. A sudden noise of a jet plane overhead, and a wee hand points out of the buggy, and upwards toward the sky.

'Meeeooooom, meeeoooooom!'

We pass the clearing which is now full of new trees; we were here last autumn planting an oak tree. I saw deer here last winter, and I worry if they will damage the trees; I would like to see them again, and then I remember an afternoon when a swallow swooped low, and my boy stopped, and watched its flight into the dark of the wood.

In the rain, we have avoided puddles; in the wind, we have pulled ourselves close to one another. In the sunshine, we have meandered, and in the ice, we have slid. We have noticed the change of seasons; my toddler learned the word for blue when the bluebells in the wood appeared; we have kicked up the autumn leaves and we have stopped to pick the daisies growing by the side of the road. I have comforted my boy as he has run out of the trees screaming from the pain of a nettle sting, and I have called him back to the road when he ran into the woods, and away from me.

When in labour, with my now sleeping baby, I walked this road in my mind. I walked this road, and ended each contraction here, by the lollipop lady, and here, at the edge of the playing fields. It was to the deer running through the clearing, to the little hedgehog in the undergrowth, to the boys reaching out for the first of the brambles, and to the swoop of the swallows, that I turned.

It is not an extraordinary place. In a land of such natural beauty, it is not one to seek out, but it is this road bordered by a wood where I walk with my children; the road on which I watch them grow, and hold their hands. Where I hear their first words, and then listen to their stories. This road, when time is on our side, where we leave and enter the wood from; Kellie Road, my favourite place; the place where my life happens. ∎

On Considering a Tumbledown at Leac na Ban

Alexander Hamilton

At a time beyond recall, a man
A man, his wife, two bairns, perhaps a dog
Came here and settled, what did they see?
I look at the wet, wet ground, the sour acid soil
What did they grow and where?
All is rush and barren hummocks
Their house is still here, what is left of it
But enough to impress, how did they raise the walls?
Look at the stones, the size of them, see that one,
      massy and defiant
Look at the heft in it, see the weight of it
There's a ton or more of rock in that one stone
And that one, and that one, such a weight of stone
      piled high
Did she help, skirts girded, hands raw? Still feeding the
      youngest
Strapped to her back, wrapped in a shawl
Were there beasts? A garron, to drag the rock,
      a primitive sledge?
How else? No wheels could take this ground
And the walls as high as his reach. So many paces
      long, so many paces wide
Was he born knowing how to gable?
Did he help his father, and gain the knowledge?
Was she the driving force, the imperative?
Enough of the rude hut, of the inadequacies
She wants a proper nest, for the quickening

Did others help with the roof? Gather the heather,
    tie down the thatch
Tamp the floor, strew myrtle and meadowsweet?
Oh the exquisite joy of that first fire, the glow on the
    walls, the light in the eye
The cry of a child, the sweet murmur of a mother
Yet none to note their passing, or if so, all record lost
But their triumph still stands, wrested with extra-
    ordinary will
Bearing witness to their existence.
So much sweat, and there must have been blood
His, hers, theirs, nourishing the ground
I understand the need for place, to be in a place,
    of a place
What was theirs is now mine
I look across their hills, into their distance
I walk on their ground
And am glad.

■

The Clyde at Rothesay Bay

Alison Clark

SOMEONE ONCE told me that the sea remembers everything and that she never forgets. The sea keeps everything she wants deep and close to her, spitting out what she doesn't. She keeps the tears of emigrating peoples and the dying breaths of sailors and throws up, on beaches thousands of miles away, everything from plastic ducks to fishing boats, to remind us, we who live on the land, that she is everywhere.

I have lived beside the River Clyde all my life. I have lived beside the upper reaches, where the smell of oil and dying vegetation hangs over everything, where the deceptively slow river has rips and undertows that can suck and kill. Floating dogs, polystyrene cups and plastic bags dance lazily on its greasy surface. Now I live on Bute – an island near its mouth, where the water around us is clear and where seals and dolphins swim. Always, always, I have looked out on the water. I used to watch my husband sail past me, years ago, on his way to the wild Arctic Ocean – watch him until I could see him no more. I would wait for the bow-wave of the ship's wash to break upon the shore and only then turn for home.

As he left on the voyages that lasted months, I, as a fearful and hopeful bride, would go to the water's edge and give the sea a small sacrifice. A token. 'It has to be just enough to hurt,' I was told. And so, one by one, I gave her what was important to me then – a whole packet of cigarettes. And with each one I threw as far as I could into the black water I prayed; 'Let this be enough for you; let my husband return to me, safe and sound.' So I kept my bargain and she kept hers.

The windows of my house here in Rothesay, the main town on Bute, look out on to the sea that takes my man from me for the greater part of every year – and yet still brings him home. I watch the dawns and the seasons turn and I watch the sea, peaceful or wild. I watch the migrating flocks of geese that fly south in the autumn and I watch the tides.

We speak to each other; the sea and me – sometimes a whisper, sometimes a howl. And thus it has always been for the wives of sailors and fishermen. We watch her closely – she that might take him from us. We cannot go far. We are rooted on the shore. We live a jealous life.

My Favourite Place? Oh yes. My favourite, my only place. ■

Arrochar
Glenn Merrilees

A mind when A wis only ten
ma faither said tae me
A'm gonna take ye fishin' son
a loch filled wi' the sea.

So we headed off tae Arrochar
a train and then a bus
an if A cast ma mind back right
there wis nearly nine o us.

Eight strong men an me a junior
Buchanan Street in line,
'A need tae dae a message,'
said Big Jock, 'if A've goat time.'

He'd been savin' up fag coupons,
he hud thousands, h''d dun weel,
he nipped in tae the exchange shoap
an goat a rod 'n' reel.

He came back in fourteen minutes
no need at all tae fuss,
eight strong men an junior
all loaded oan the bus.

Oor bus reached its destination
but gee whizz whit a hike!
we hud tae cairy aw that gear
A wished A'd brought ma bike.

So we goat oorsel's a nice flat spot
a place tae pitch oor tent
then seven o those big strong men
doon tae the pub they went.

So me an dear auld Walker
were left tae watch the stuff
we gethered loads an loads o wid
until we hud enough.

So we goat an early night in
nine folk inside a tent,
leave early in the mornin'
well that wis their intent.

They'd booked two boats tae take us oot
tae fish that deep Loch Long
'We'll come back wi' loads o fish,'
by god they werenae wrong.

Alas A couldnae make it
A wis afraid tae board that boat
so A stayed wi' dear auld Walker
An that goat ma faither's goat.

A wis young an A wis frightened
an A could smell that salty sea
visions o fallin' overboard
hud goat a grip oan me.

So off they trudged without me
eight oors later they came back
each man hud loads o mackerel
in an overflowin' sack.

So they pit them in the river
thinkin' that'll keep them coolish
but hindsight is a funny thing
cause it turnt oot that wis foolish.

We went tae bed, goat snuggled in
A prayed fur peaceful dreams
but ma sleep wis interrupted
by the sound o big Bert's screams.

A spring tide sprung upon us
river backed up all around
panic in the darkness
as we searched for drier ground.

Situation worsenin'
an this is whit wis said
'Somebody pick the wee man up,
it's far too deep tae wade.'

We made it tae the roadside
tae wan o many bridges
frozen cauld an soakin' wet
gettin' chewed tae death by midges.

Moon emerged fae behind a cloud
an eerie sight we saw
bags o fish hud disappeared
an belongins washed awa'.

We stood there fur six hoors
we'd await the ebbin' tide,
midges drank three pints o blood,
nowhere we could hide.

We goat back tae oor campsite
a place we couldnae stay
everythin' wis soakin'
half it washed away.

Some o them they humphed an' hawed
an others they just tutted
A felt like the mackerel though
cause A wis bloody gutted.

■

Edinburgh Waverley Railway Station

Frances Hider

TODAY, EDINBURGH Waverley is as gloomy as wartime blackout. Shrouds – to facilitate refurbishment – cover the thirteen acres of glass roof keeping light out and darkness in. Standing on Platform 19 waiting for the London train, I'm reminded of Ern.

Ern swore he'd never forget me and promised we'd meet in Edinburgh, at the station, when the time was right. I was sure he meant it.

Ern was five foot two and if he were here now would be lost in the crowd. Lost, that is, until he opened his mouth and let forth a comforting Canadian drawl. Ern had a voice as loud as a klaxon, a big nose and three fingers on his left hand; 'tabernacle' was his favourite swear word.

I should mention at this point, we're a family of first namers. Ern was always Ern. There are no Gramps, Grannies, Nannies, Grandpas or – in Ern's case – Granddads in our family.

Ern was a war veteran. He would hold up his three fingers and fashion an uneven V. 'Victory,' he'd say, 'and long live the other side.'

He passed through the station in 1952; London to Edinburgh Waverley and return; he was on his honeymoon. For Annie – Gran to you – it was a second marriage. But for Ern, a man of secrets, it could have been a first, second or third for all anyone knew. Being Canadian, Ern threw his ticket out of the train window

59

– apparently it was the norm over there – and had to demand another if he was to get home. While waiting he was told the story of the infamous spy Werner Walti and William Merrilees – aka Wee Willie the pocket detective – and missed his train.

In September 1940, Werner Walti AKA Robert Petter also missed his train. In his pocket he had a single ticket from Edinburgh to London along with a Mauser automatic pistol, a flick-knife, a compass and the wartime tools of espionage. He was arrested at the left luggage office by Sergeant Merrilees who with the flair of Sherlock, and disguised as a porter, had lain in wait. Merrilees went on to be Chief Constable; Walti was hung.

Ern didn't see action. He sang in the Salvation Army and played the drums; he wore his uniform with pride. Ern was no stranger to hope and glory. Hopefully he loved Annie, but Ern also loved the station. He loved knowing he could catch a train which would take him north or south.

I love the station because once Ern's Canadian twang echoed in the Victorian cupola as he demanded a new ticket; his slicked back hair reflected a ghostly green in the filtered light. How Ern lost his fingers is a mystery. Ern turned out to be AKA someone else altogether; luckily it wasn't a hangable offence. Annie flushed her wedding ring down the toilet and that was that. No one ever again said tabernacle.

I'll never forget Ern. When the shrouding is removed from the overhead glass the station will return to normal. But Edinburgh Waverley will always remind me of Ern and of promises never meant to be broken. ∎

Strachan's Bus

Sandra Murray

CLIMBING THE high metal steps of the red Strachan's bus, mother shooing me along the aisle, I would choose a seat by the window on the right-hand side. It had to be on that side so we could wave to Rob Roy when the bus drove over the bridge in Culter.

Sitting down in my best green polka dot dress, I could feel the itching start at the back of my knees where the moquette fabric of the seats rubbed against my skin. The seat at the front, behind the driver, was where the conductress would sit chatting to him between the stops. On the opposite side the front two seats would be stacked from the floor up with misshapen parcels, crates and piles of string-tied newspapers. All to be dropped off at farm gates on our journey up the Braemar road.

Leaving the town behind us, we would natter away about all and everything we could see from our window. Then the conductress would start taking fares. I so wanted to be a conductress when I grew up, just like the one on this bus. To my young mind, she had a very important job punching out tickets from the silver machine sitting on her hip. She knew exactly what the fare cost from one bend in the road to the other and would deposit the money into the large leather saddlebag which was slung across her body. Tilting her bag towards her she would have a good rake inside for the correct change. The front of her black shirt gleamed with polished badges and some blonde hair poked out from under her black cap. Ruby red lipstick completed the look and gave her the appearance of a film star, like Kim Novak, whose posters adorned my uncle's bedroom wall.

The driver always knew where to stop on the road and when the conductress picked up her first parcel, my guessing game would start. What was inside? A pair of shoes, a fancy ornament or games compendium? As the bus slowed down she would descend a step and slide open the concertina door with her free hand. Handing it over to whoever was waiting at the roadside, I imagined their delight at receiving the long-awaited goods. Sometimes they would return the favour and another mysterious bundle would be taken on board, bound for delivery further along the road or the depot in Aberdeen for despatching on a different bus.

If it was a blustery day I'd stare out the window at the clouds scudding across the sky, then follow their shadows on the fields below. The River Dee would trail us like a black snake lying parallel to our route through the countryside, sometimes hidden in the undergrowth and other times laid bare for all to see.

Approaching Aboyne Loch I'd kneel on my seat, neck craned trying to spot the water skiers. Stopping outside Strachan's general store in Aboyne to unload more packages, the passengers would spill out of the bus to stretch their legs. I'd enter the shop and buy my favourite icicle – a strawberrry Mivvi.

Passing through Dinnet I always looked forward to Loch Kinord coming into view – my dad had rowed me over to one of the small islets when we had camped nearby. I'll never forget the response we got from the colony of birds nesting there! I still have nightmares.

Next stop was Ballater where the bus would head for the depot and drive straight inside the garage. Again the passengers would exit the bus for ten minutes and Mum would take me the short distance to Leith's bakery to buy a pineapple tart for our tea. Once heated up in the Calor Gas oven at the caravan, it would be transformed into a deluxe pudding when a tin of Carnation Milk was poured over it! I can taste it now. Oh joy! Before leaving the garage, yet more boxed goods were added to the depleted stock of parcels. Empty seats were scattered about the bus as folks headed for home and hikers left for the hills or hostels. Just a few more miles to go for us.

Another delivery stop was the Coilacriech Inn and I'd look across the bus for a glimpse of Lochnagar. Soon the chimneys of Tomidhu would come into view. Who would be first to see the smoke rise from them? This game was played between us on every trip. Standing up I'd ring the bell and we'd make our way to the front. The driver would nod in acknowledgement and crank the gears bringing the bus to a stop. With a smile from Kim Novak, we'd climb down the metal steps and I'd hear the dull thud of the doors closing on my favourite place. ∎

Flow Country

LM Morgan

I am thinking of this on our drive up the coast
over the Cromarty Bridge, where I look from the window
to see a strip of shining sea, mirror-white,
following as we drive across the firth.
It is not on this sunlit water but the loch-strewn
plains of the Flow Country
where my thoughts rest, weltering in the still
waters of a blue bog, tall reeds
pricking through the white clouds of its reflection.

Another bridge, only here at Dornoch the tide is out,
the sand stretching out into the summer dusk like
    salt flats.
Here and there lie pools of water tinged mauve,
    while out to sea
it is as white and intangible as heaven.
I have made this journey many times,
first in your R-reg Transit, and now in the silver
    Volkswagen,
but always loaded with your surfboards
and a yellowing Silentnight mattress,
my books piled about the floor on the passenger's side
(usually some Sylvia Plath which I will insist
on reading aloud even though you hate it).

In the hills around Golspie, I see a cottage,
one small window lit, and this is what I am thinking,
while you drive up the coast, in the falling light:
one day, the mattress – the one your upstairs

neighbour gave us,
seven years ago, when we were just kids –
will be replaced with a sofa, crates of dishes,
        our table and chairs,
and we will carry it all
north, where we belong, and the books in the floorwell
will be lined up on a pine bookcase
in the dark hall of some low-roofed cottage.

The road bobs and dips so we feel more like a ship
        at sea,
and just as we reach Portgower it drops
into the rocks and surf, as we round
the bend into the village.
We cut across the Flow on the back road to Melvich,
forty miles of single track. White moths
from the moorland flutter past in the headlights,
and it is here, beneath Ben Griam Beg,
volcano-like, pointing up into the clouds,
that we see Loch an Ruathair, shining
like a shard of moon half sunk in the bog.

The sky seems bigger up here – deeper, wider –
as though viewed through a fisheye lens.
And now, as you drive still, I am thinking of tomorrow,
when we will walk on the beach,
and the turquoise water will be cut
with ice-white froth.
And we will stand by the water's edge and listen –
because we have nothing more pressing to do –
to the roll and wash
of the waves, the slop and the fizz
when they break on sand the colour of wet bricks.

In the brightly lit lounge of the Halladale Inn,
where the smell of boiled tatties starches the air,
a man leans his elbow on the bar,
he wants to know how far we've come and where
        we're stopping,
and I am rapt in the lilt and burr of his voice.
This is how it sounds to my Lowlander ear –
It is the tap of loose shutters and the wind in the lock.
It is the skipping of a schoolgirl and the flare of her skirt.
It is the click of knitting needles and the draw of the wool.

At Strathy, we pull into the car park above the dunes,
parking up near the stone dyke of the graveyard –
        where tomorrow
you will hang your wet towel and I will pray
the dead do not mind – and we step out into the cool
night breeze, to brush our teeth in the long grass.
All the clouds have gone and you pull me close,
tell me to look up.
Night is different in the far north.
We stand there for a long time, cradled in each other's
        silence
and by the sound of the waves breaking, far, far, below.

■

From Iona, With Answered Prayers

Keith Roberts

WE HAD watched the catch being landed earlier in the day. Drizzled with garlic butter, the langoustines stared up at us, fresh enough to almost breathe. A warming island malt, a ten-year-old from Tobermory, rinsed the palate. Through the glass we watched as the ferry struggled to approach the same jetty that had welcomed the prawns hours earlier; the same one from which we had disembarked as dawn broke. The storm had risen through the afternoon; rain lashed the white beaches; wind whipped the waves into meringues. The ferry disappeared into a trough and my stomach began to fear the short crossing that lay ahead, assuming the boat would eventually dock.

But for all that we had enjoyed peace and solitude of the type we knew we could find nowhere else. We had escaped and we had found, and we had hope once more; just the two of us.

A few weeks earlier we had been three, but it was not to be. This time the miscarriage came with shattering news. It told of chromosome disorders, horrific disfigurement, short life. Perhaps we were fortunate that there would be no life, but the revelation of what may lie ahead shook us to the core. So we escaped.

From our weekend base outside Bunessan, on Mull, we followed the familiar road to the ferry at Fionnphort. Across the sound Iona waited, arms open and welcoming as always. It was not a day for a nap on the

White Strand, for it was November, chilly and windswept, and the ferries were on the winter timetable.

I headed for the Bay at the Back of the Ocean, lost in my own thoughts, buffeted by the wind. Crossing the golf course, where the hardy island sheep grazed the machair, I reached the cockle strand and gazed out into nothing. Further west lay Boston. Waves crashed on rocks.

Gilly headed in the opposite direction, through the village, to the abbey, as I knew she would. Candles were lit. It was not for me. I'm someone who reserves candles for blackouts. I walked thrice round Sidhean Mor, the Big Fairy Mound, and tramped through the wet to rise to the summit of Dun I. Gulls rode thermals; Highland cattle turned their long-haired docks to the wind; the corncrake had long since left. All around islands rose and fell in the swell. Of the Treshnish Isles only the Dutchman's Cap remained on the horizon. And from Staffa the overture thundered from the cave. I could almost hear it.

We met in the nunnery, where pockets of pink and yellow flowers clung to gaps in the ancient stones. Sheltering, we shared a flask of chicken soup, and rested against the south wall of the refectory, unaware then what lay in the ancient walls above us. Tears rolled, though I swore the wind could not be blamed. Denial.

Through the clouds a ray broke above the abbey, the tower limned in autumn light.

'I'm finding my peace,' she said, eventually.

I was still angry, but calming as exhaustion set in and the mud dried on my boots. Guilt it was; all those years of smoking. Now it might be too late. The years had passed as inexorably as the waves crashed on the shore. But the indifference had disappeared, replaced with desire and yearning. I had been found wanting, incomplete, incapable. She didn't deserve such pain.

'That's good my love, Iona always helps.'

And so it was that we found ourselves at table in the Martyrs' Bar, fed and watered, as the ferry struggled. There was time for another dram, and a last walk, up to the tiny school, past the nunnery, but not long enough to reach the graves of our ancient kings in the abbey grounds. Across the sound the red granite cliffs of Mull took the setting sun, seeming larger and nearer.

The ferry made the slipway, engine running, her stay brief. We had to run, together, hand in hand, bedraggled and soaked. The return to Fionnphort was not pleasant, but then it never was. Normally a mere ten minutes or so, the crossing was eternal. The tears ran again, but they often did, leaving Iona.

It was later, weeks later, that I learned of the sheela-na-gig. Apparently sheelas were not uncommon. Many buildings hosted them. But on a nunnery, in this centre of Christianity? We had rested beneath female genitalia, made of stone, an ancient fertility symbol.

It may have been the candle, or the fairies, but whatever it was the family is now complete. Nine months later the dam burst, and within another year or so we were four, in rude health. She always believed, I always doubted. Iona healed. And every time we pass that Bunessan cottage, eyes sparkle. ■

Island of (South) Rona

Valerie McIlreavy

you are the leaving of Portree and the white painted
     arrow on the rock at Acarsaid Mhor;
you are the sunset flooding Trotternish and the
     dancing light on Storr;
you are the Danish Princess, finally at rest with her
     Greek lover up at Blarain;
you are the elusive otter and the soaring sea eagle
     at Acarsaid Thioram;
you are the dark and wild water of Caol Rona on an
     autumn day;
you are the women carrying the seaweed up from the
     shore at Dry Harbour while their men were away
     at war;
you are the close encounter with the basking shark –
     magical and life-changing;
you are the ruins of Am Teampuil at the south, where
     the monk once lived;
you are the tangy rhubarb and the sweet brambles by
     the old schoolhouse at Dry Harbour;
you are the oldest rocks in western Europe and the
     Lewisian gneiss;
you are the tales of the furtive smugglers, of their
     hidden whisky and their illicit stills;
you are grey seals, cormorants and deep diving
     gannets in the Sound of Raasay;
you are every single season in one glorious day, you
     are the joy of island weather;
you are the red deer stag on the rock above Red
     Alex's crumbled home;

you are the inspiring, revealing and magical power
of a wild place;

you are the welcome at Rona Lodge and Bill's famous
oatcakes;

you are the lobsters and the crabs caught in the creels
at Dry Harbour;

you are the sweet scent of bog myrtle and the subtle
notes of heather;

you are Calum MacLeod of Raasay, who (as well as
building his road),

kept the Rona Light well supplied;

you are the views over Torridon from the track and
Beinn Alligin in the distance;

you are the marsh marigold, the ragged robin and the
yellow primrose growing in abundance;

you are the pod of dolphins seen from the boat and
the minke whales;

you are the emotion of Duncan MacSwan, revisiting
the place of his birth and childhood after forty-
two years away;

you are Eilean Tighe, Garbh Eilean and little Eilean
Fhraoich;

you are the getting 'drunk' (on the mind blowing
360 degree views from up) on Meall Acarsaid;

you are the natural reverence of Church Cave and the
quiet dignity of the stone 'pulpit';

you are Captain Otter's letter to Alan Stevenson in
praise of Janet MacKenzie who kept a light in her
cottage window to warn sailors of the rocks at
Acarsaid Mhor;

you are the sharp winter wind that cuts over Doire na
Guaille and the thick snow lying in the
abandoned houses there;

you are Flora MacRae and her two brothers working
        their little bit of land;
you are Roderick MacKay bravely giving evidence
        to the Napier Commission;
you are the men who left Dry Harbour in May 1921
        to reclaim their lands on Raasay;
you are the sizzling mackerel in the pan – caught only
        an hour ago;
you are the shimmering rainbow at Acarsaid Thioram;
you are nine hundred and thirty hectares of history
        and life;
you are the centre of the universe;
you are in my heart and in my soul forever;
you are my favourite place;
you are the magical, mystical Island of Rona

■

Ardencraig Gardens

Ann Foster

THE AWARD-winning Victorian Garden is always a source of pleasure to all who step inside. The walled garden contains Victorian greenhouses bursting to overflowing with beautiful pot plants and of course there is the garden itself. Raised beds ablaze with colour, ponds splashed with water lilies, goldfish lazily swimming by and my favourite, the aviaries. The aviaries are so full of life; finches, parakeets, doves, starlings all whistle and hum with the pure joy of being alive.

By day this is a busy place. Gardeners are working; children excitedly talking to the birds; plant experts studying the colour schemes, taking notes, making sketches, and others who just come to sit quietly with their thoughts, a place for healing.

By night the garden is a very different place. It no longer belongs to us. The light is different, the plants are no longer vibrant, the large greenhouses groan and creak as the temperature changes. I feel like a trespasser and I know I am not wanted, that the garden is hostile.

I unlock the large green door, the original door, 100 years old. I turn the key in my hand and wonder how many hands have held this key. I step inside and stand perfectly still, viewing my surroundings. The pot plants that are housed in long rows in the greenhouses stand to attention, like soldiers on parade at a military funeral, no longer cheerful but somehow sinister. The glass roof closes, making a groaning noise that makes me start. I force myself to stay calm.

I scan the gardens, my eyes travelling over the flower beds and aviaries. The birds are quiet. Everything seems normal. I listen hard. Nothing.

I check on the birds and all is well; I collect my watering can and start to fill it from the hose on the wall. A shadow, a movement, catches my eye. Someone is in the greenhouse. I can see the shape of a tall man moving along the rows of plants. My hand shakes and I spill water on to the path. Turning the hose off I enter the side door of the greenhouse.

Whoever or whatever it is, is moving away from me, always just out of sight.

I call out; 'Who is there?' I hurry through the long corridors of the greenhouse in pursuit. I hear the outside door bang. Whoever it is has gone outside into the garden. I double back. I should be able to cut him off but when I reach the garden no one is there.

This is not the first time this has happened to me. Was someone playing a trick, or was my imagination working overtime?

I sit down on the nearest bench, for my legs are trembling. From here I have a full view of the garden and there is definitely no one here but me. I walk around and check the gates. Could I have left the outside door unlocked and had someone come in? But all the doors are secure.

Then I see it and my heart gives a thud. The spilled water on the path. Someone has walked through it for there is a large footprint. Someone had walked through the puddle I had made with the hose, but walked to where? There is no door to go through, just a large brick wall.

Is this place haunted or am I going quietly mad?

I think back to the other occasions. Like the time I was working in the aviary when I heard someone walking on the gravel path outside. At first I thought one of the gardeners had come back but when I looked out there was no one there. Then there was the smell. I was convinced I could smell cigar smoke in the greenhouses and there was the night when I heard soft whistling. I shivered; perhaps I should only come here during the day when the gardens are busy with people.

I pick up my watering can and go back to the aviary. I start feeding the birds. Percy my Senegal parrot is sitting on my shoulder, supervising my work as usual, when suddenly he takes off and flies to the far corner of the outside flight. I am surprised and uneasy as he never normally leaves me.

Percy is my parrot and he is in love with me. He has eyes for me and me alone; he sits on my shoulder, preens my hair and openly adores me. He also talks in a high pitched female voice which must be mine.

I call him back, but he ignores me. I follow him down the flight, stopping to watch in amazement.

Percy is looking into the garden and away from me; he is in full courtship display but to whom or what? For there is nothing and no one to be seen.

He is doing his best to make someone fall in love with him: he is seeing something that I cannot.

'What are you doing, you silly bird?' I call to him. Percy turns to look at me and in a clear, deep, man's voice he says, 'Get Out'. ■

Clouds

Louise Hopkins

Under the Alders Amongst the Grasses by the River in Yarrow

Helen Douglas

Andrew and Inge at the Kitchen Table: 160 Hill Street

Alasdair Gray

WE WERE LIKE THIS IN 1966

When We Were Kings

Phil Stephen

T IS 1984, I am twelve and I live in a world where danger does not exist. Trees are meant to be climbed, knees are meant to be skinned and hands are constantly grubby. I am twelve and life is for living.

Today my best friend and I are off for a river adventure, so essential preparation is necessary, beginning with lunch. As I live in Scotland I make a piece, not a sandwich, and here I show my willingness to dice with danger. I open the bread bin and pull out the plain white bread, free from Omega 3s and without a trace of oats or seeds, and smear on some soft butter (both sides) before reaching for the jam. Homemade raspberry jam, straight from the fields of Balgove Farm, slapped generously on the bread; by the time lunchtime has come around the warmth of my lunchbox will have cooked my piece into a white square doughnut of delight. I pack the rest of my bag and tell my mum what time I will be home then it's off to the shed. My parents do not own a car and therefore my other source of freedom lies in front of me, the product of a hard summer's work in the berry fields. A Kalkhoff ten-speed racer with ram-horn handlebars, well-worn brake blocks and shiny silver gears which sit frighteningly on the down frame.

Struan pulls up at the gate. His parents are teachers and he has a fifteen-speed Raleigh, mine however is faster. Neither of us cares as we are more intent on reaching our destination today. Once again dicing with death we cycle off without helmets, a thing of the future, off up Nursery Road taking a left into the main road passing Kuilinski's Corner Shop (home of the world famous ice cream 'Can you fill my mum's tub please?') before we head off over the Vicky Bridge and out to Hillside. We stretch on, standing up in our saddles as Hillside approaches and the long slow climb to the top makes our bikes swish from side to side as we try to maintain our speed. A right turn across the road at the top, travelling slowly, gathering our breath before we hit Deadman's Dive and the road to Martin's Den.

Turning a corner we slam into our highest gears and pump our legs furiously as we hit top speed, hunched over like a pair of future Chris Hoys with elbows tucked in. Our fear knows no bounds as we hurtle down at breakneck speed, dodging potholes and screaming with joy. Only at twelve can you feel this much pleasure, and of course nobody is coming the other way.

And at last we are there coming abruptly to a halt before the cool clear water of the North Esk and the spot we call Martin's Den. Rummaging through our packs we pull out our lunches, pairs of cut-off jeans, t-shirts and battered old river shoes. (No one likes crossing a river in bare feet!) With no one around we strip off and change and the day is ours. We set about edging into the river talking about nothing (and girls) trying to ignore the growing sense of trepidation as the water approaches waist height, then it's a brave and furious launch of arms and legs as we shock our bodies into an attempt to equalise with the freezing cold. We swim free of lanes, chlorine, bright coloured plastic and unrestricted by coloured rubber bands. Life hands us a moment in time; sharp, clear and joyous. Ropes drip from trees at the water's edge and we launch ourselves into the air screaming like Tarzan, we run low to the bank swinging in a wide arc causing circular waves to rise in the river. Stones fly across, skipping and jumping from bank to bank as we aim for fish, birds or rabbits. Dams are made as sections of the river are diverted and changed before the minimal resistance is washed away. This is abandoned freedom of the sort only small boys can experience.

We break for lunch and in a time before suncream was invented we lie bare-chested on our towels gazing at the clouds in the bluest of skies. The warmth brings the smell of riverbank weeds and grass wafting across, mixing with the distinctive popcorn aroma of fresh oilseed rape. The hayfever I will develop as an adult does not even blink at this cornucopia of pollen. Bees buzz and the odd daddy longlegs causes me to jump as it tries to climb over my damp wet hair. Strangely I don't remember a single midgie. Pieces come out of the bag and are demolished as we eye the jumping fish, knowing all the while they will never be caught. The warm diluting juice leaves a tacky taste in my mouth and I wish for more of these summer days. Lying still in the sun I let the day sink in and despite my age I know there will never again be a time like this.

Where the hours go I can never remember but soon my Timex says 3.30 and reluctantly we must head off. Climbing back on our bikes with bags of wet clothes, the journey home seems longer. We constantly glance back as if our place, our favourite place, will disappear. When we reach the top of Deadman's Dive we stop with a long look back.

'Hey Struan, how about tomorrow?'

'Yeah, mate.'

I have been back to Martin's Den many times as an adult. The road does not change and the fishing cobble remains tied up in the same position. The river is as cool and clean as ever and the popcorn oilseed rape lingers in the background. It remains my favourite place frozen in time, in the summer of 1984, when we were kings. ■

Leith, 1974

Marianne Paget

MARNIE, SEVEN years old, steps out from Linksview House, the high rise where she lives cheek by jowl with her friends, slipping skinny arms through letter boxes on the doors of long low landings to break into empty houses to play, sitting on cold stone balconies shrieking in delight and disgust over bags of buckies. Marnie turns right and watches her legs kick into the milk white morning haar as she walks. She imagines she's a pirate lost at sea or a princess trapped in a cloudy tower. She stops. There's a distant pattering; growing louder, coming her way. Her heart drums. She grips the coins her mum gave her for messages. Dark shapes stir in the haar ahead. Then – an explosion: her friends, feral and full of energy, burst from the fog, faces ruddy as sailors, eyes sparkling.

'Harris's smashed the pigeon's eggs. We're gonnae kill'um.' Franny, Linda, Craig, Monkey and Wee Stevie flash by, disappearing back into the haar.

Marnie's heart hammers. The coins gouge her palm. Messages or the fight? Messages or the fight? There's a click-thwop sound of a window opening, and the Bay City Rollers bridge to the chorus: Shaaaaaang-a-Lang, Shang-a-lang, Shang-a-lang, Shang-a-lang. Marnie howls a battle cry and runs with the gang.

They charge through the vennel under the flats into a dazzling light. The tower block barricades the haar from its south side and here the sun shines on the vast slabbed square spread out beneath their homes.

The day glitters: glass smashed on concrete, webs spun on railings – and the promise of a fight.

They push down the stone steps to the precinct.

'Split up,' Monkey shouts, veering towards Giles Street, Craig on his tail.

'C'mon.' Franny leads the rest of the gang to the garages where they toe away crumbling brick to climb onto the roofs, Linda giving Wee Stevie a footie.

'See 'um?' he asks.

A car below coughs into life and a radio kicks in. The Carpenters are on Top of the World. Marnie looks around. To her right, the Banana Flats – bandit territory for Linksview House kids. Behind her, still haar-bound, the Adventure Playground and the docks.

'The Links,' she shouts.

Everyone cheers, skitters to roof edges and dreeps onto grass-fringed paving. Marnie leads them towards St Mary's. 'This way.'

They scuttle through the yard between the squat church and the statue of God stretching out His arms as if to say 'What the...?' Marnie keeps her head down, refusing to meet His burning stare.

They hit the Links running, throw themselves onto the ground and roll around laughing, exhausted. Here is a world of brilliant colour, bright as poster paints, a wash of blue sky over thick brushed green grass. The air is clean and fresh, the earth cool and wet. It smells of the Earth. It smells of real. The July sun burns off the last of the haze and slowly they relax to the hypnotic sound of distant traffic.

Monkey and Craig jump off the giant anchor in the middle of the Kirkgate as Marnie's posse arrives.

'Found 'um?' Franny asks.

Monkey shakes his head. 'Craig's got money for swedgers but.'

Suddenly they're all starving and the fight can wait. They whoop and gallop towards the sweetie shop on Henderson Street where the shopkeeper counts up in half and whole pences as Craig fills a white paper bag to bursting. Then, sticking to Craig like seagulls to a chip bag, they squeeze out of the narrow shop doorway, squawking all the way back to the rubble of the Adventure Playground. Craig dishes out sweets and they make a feast from stones and sticks, dust and spit and pretend-sip from an empty Tennent's lager can, sniggering at 'Lovely' of the day, topless Tina.

Linda jumps up. 'Comin' tae look for Harris?'

Halfway down Water Street, Monkey pulls loose boards off the doorway to an old whisky bond. The gang snake up a circular staircase to the top floor and skirt charcoaled floorboards which point jagged fingers towards a hole in the centre of the room.

Outside again, the sun has gone. A breeze, briny from the Firth of Forth, dry-scrubs their skin and matts their hair. They head for the vantage point of Lamb's House; zigzagged turrets edging its red slate roof, tiny cross-hatched windows peppering its tall white walls. They clamber onto bins and leap onto porticos like a litter of kittens and somehow make it to the top of the perilously steep roof.

'Harris!' Craig yells, pointing into the cobbled lane below.

Harris runs full pelt towards them, waving and pointing towards the Forth. 'There's a dead body in the docks.'

His crime is instantly forgotten. The gang slide

down the roof, drop to the ground and race with him down Shore Place. Seagulls shriek, circling a pub blasting out Terry Jacks' 'Seasons in the Sun'. They round the corner, Marnie colliding with the first of the night's prossies. Curses follow the friends downriver to where a group of older kids huddle together at the dock's edge. The new arrivals stop short, exchange looks. Marnie licks her salty lips with a kipper-dry tongue then walks towards the huddle. With every step she takes over the shiny cobbles she imagines she's shrinking. She imagines the ghostly tentacles of a sea monster reaching up from the dank water, wrapping round her ankles, pulling her in, pulling her under. She holds her breath then peers into the thick black soup of the Water of Leith as the sea-haar rolls in and engulfs her once more. ∎

Mobile Library Man

Howard Swindells

THIS IS A song I wrote about being the driver of a mobile library van. The mobile library operates throughout the Highlands but Assynt is the region that I particularly love. The song refers to many places and many people that I have met as part of this job. I have sung this song in various places including a meeting of mobile library drivers. It has always been well received. I hope that you like it.

I am the mobile library man
I drive the mobile library van
I bring you books wherever I can
To Lairg, Drumbeg and Badnaban

Falls of Shin, Clachtoll beach
You'd think these places out of reach
But the yellow van it must get through
To bring some sex and violence out to you
I drive by mountain loch and glen
Down single track roads and back again
And the only thing that makes me curse
Is meeting a camper van that can't reverse

I am the mobile library man ...

I think of where I used to be
In a primary class of thirty-three
I'd lose my temper every day
And wish that I could simply run away
But now I drive this big yellow bus
And shelving books is the biggest fuss
Along the byways roaming free
This really is the only job for me

I am the mobile library man …

When I beep my horn I'm at your gate
Come on out I'm running late
Then at Mrs Gunn's I stop for tea
With cakes and scones and jam she's made for me
Then off again along the shore
Take Mr Parker's books on war
Then Kinbrace school, but no need for fright
There's only three kids there so that's alright

I am the mobile library man …

Mrs Leith comes out in slippers
scours the shelves for bodice rippers
Jamie and his brother Neil
Bring the books in an old wheelbarrow with a squeaky
        wheel
Mrs Ross says I've baked a cake
Can you take it down the road to my brother Jake
If you do I'll give you a chocolate bun
You can't call this job work it's so much fun

I am the mobile library man …

Last week I had a bit of a glitch
And dropped a front wheel in a ditch
Behind my head I heard a roar
When I looked, 500 books were on the floor
I nearly drove straight to the tip
It was less like a library more like a skip
It took five hours to get things straight
I'm driving slower now so I might be late

I am the mobile library man …

■

The Wonder of You

Kenny Pieper

A YOUNG BOY of about six sits on a wall, swinging his legs. He is shivering and doesn't understand why he has been dragged out into the cold by his father and uncle but the big bottle of Tizer and quarter of cola cubes certainly help matters. He is somewhere he cannot quite comprehend. Vaguely aware of the twenty-two men kicking a ball about somewhere over to his side, he is, however, far more interested in the long row of funny wee blue cars which have driven towards him and are now lined up facing the twenty-two men kicking a ball about somewhere over to his side. His dad and uncle secretly sip beer from cans which disappear back into their jacket pockets now and again. He cannot possibly copy them with his Tizer. Asking for trouble. But little does he know that this would be the first visit in a lifetime of visits he would make to this huge, strange place.

Fast forward seven or eight years and the same boy, now a spotty teenager, is standing, still freezing, slightly back from the same spot. Old enough to come and watch Partick Thistle on his own, he has to accept a lifetime of solitary confinement and afternoons alone as his friends have opted for the all-too-safe havens of Ibrox and Parkhead. Even at thirteen years old, he is aware of the choice he has made, the difficult social situations which may arise, the difference. He has his doubts at times. He has brought those friends along before now, hopeful of a miraculous conversion which never comes. One game was dreadful, the other a victory which caused no end of embarrassment when they played Cliff Richard's 'Congratulations' over the tannoy. But he was at Firhill, his comfort zone and he knew even then that it would always be that way.

Another eight years pass. School is well gone and he pays his own way. But he still walks alone. Home and away now but things never replace that warm familiar feeling as he walks through the turnstiles and the stands in the same place. He takes every defeat personally; it ruins his evening and possibly his Sunday too. Relationships are made and lost on the strength of a Saturday afternoon and he knows that is wrong but he can't help it. Firhill on a Saturday is the only place he can find a place for that misplaced passion. The regrets, the possibilities of an alternative to Firhill have been considered and dismissed long ago. This is a part of who he is and will be. It feels good.

Ten years later. The boy within the man has lived his life elsewhere. But still the sight of the Firhill flood-lights as he walks up Maryhill Road causes him to swallow a tear and fight the tingle down his spine. The people have changed but the place remains the same. The onslaught of middle age witnesses some success. Lambie returns. Championships arrive. Firhill comes alive again. And so does his passion. The one and only time he would take a woman to Firhill would be to share that passion with the woman with whom he would spend his life. One who tolerates and under-stands, to a degree. The special one in the special place. An unexpected phone call from his brother results in a closer relationship than either of them could ever have imagined when they were younger. Firhill brings them together.

And so to 2012. The old place has just reached its century, eh? That young boy of six wouldn't have understood, wouldn't have cared. The man who he would grow into has a season ticket now and doesn't take it quite so seriously any more. However, Firhill means more to him now than ever before. A lifetime of this one constant, regular Saturday afternoon fix means that he couldn't contemplate ever watching Partick Thistle play anywhere else. If Firhill goes, that'll be it. And he'll stand and watch the bulldozers and weep. Weep for a lifetime of love and passion and obsession. And you're always there. To lend a hand in everything I do. That's the wonder. The wonder of you. ■

The United Colours
of Cumnock

Jim Monaghan

My town is a green town, but it's not a 'fuck the
    queen' green town,
it's a tree in every scene town,
wae gairdens freshly dug.
That's green that pours through every crack,
through pavements, viaducts, fitba' parks,
where men who suffer heart attacks
go walks wae three-leg dugs.

My town is a blue town, a 'who the fuck are you' town,
a 'what school did you go to' town
and 'are you one of us?'
That's blue that seeps through doors and walls,
fae pubs and bookies, village halls,
where men would guard old Derry's walls,
instead o' guarding us.

My town was once a red town, another miner dead town,
a men who fought and bled town,
wae brave and stalwart wives.
That's red that came fae meeting rooms,
fae folk that worked the pumps and looms,
when burgh bands played different tunes,
and we marched for better lives.

But now my town's a grey town, a fifty miles a day town,
a watch life slip away town,
a tunnel wae nae light.

That's grey that weeps fae dying eyes,
bewildered parents, children's cries,
wae skinny arms and stick-like thighs,
and nae strength left to fight.

■

The Louisa Mine

Lorraine Luescher

SOMETIMES, walking in the mist and the fading light on this remote and unremarkable hill, a faint but distinctive aroma of pipe smoke pervades the air, the suggestion of a crunch of heavy boots on the rough track and the clink of a horse's harness is just discernible. A man of indeterminate age in a heavy plaid coat, his head bent, passes below, drifting in and out of the mist, scarcely distinguishable from the watery landscape. And then the mist closes in and he is gone.

This is Glendinning in the early twenty-first century, an area of rolling hills and foaming burns in the Southern Uplands of Scotland, sparsely inhabited now only with sheep and the shepherds who tend them, but once the site of an eighteenth century antimony mine known as The Louisa Mine.

I am drawn again and again to this special place. It would be difficult to imagine any greater solitude and yet there is a sense of comfortable companionship all about me. More – there is a feeling of timelessness, an affinity with past inhabitants, a oneness with the landscape. Am I alone? Maybe. But lonely? Never. Here you can be a philosopher, you can examine and untangle the complex array of issues that plague ordinary life, and you can find a sense of perspective that seems to elude you in other environments.

The landscape, sculpted and moulded by the great upheavals of land mass during the Ice Age tens of thousands of years ago, has changed little with the passage of time. And from earliest times hardy and resilient settlers have scratched an existence among these hills, leaving intriguing traces of their habitations and their farming systems, their endeavours and their industriousness.

The earliest settlers in the area would have been hunter gatherers followed by the herdsmen and farmers of the Neolithic Age. Life in those times would have been harsh, ruled by superstition and ritual. Early settlements dating back to the Iron Age were invariably situated defensively, never far from water, often with livestock enclosures, hut circles, and rig and furrow cultivations. Much later during the turbulent Middle Ages, these early settlements became the fortified stronghold of the feuding clans. It is hard to place these strange random traces of human habitation on the timeline of civilisation, but the footprint of thousands of years of hill dwellers remains indelibly implanted on this remote landscape. And I am here today, my small footprint added to those who have gone before.

The old abandoned mine belonged to the age of enlightenment when boundaries were pushed beyond anything previously imagined. Forty miners laboured to dig the ore with only the most basic of tools and equipment, living in bothy accommodation with peat for fuel, candles for light, and books on history and sermons for the enrichment of their souls. The mine, when you come upon it, is almost obscured by vegetation. The high level shaft, a jagged black hole draped with ferns and heather, has been driven horizontally into the rock face. Inside, water seeps from the rock surface and flows down the calcite-coated walls, with small coated pebbles looking like sugared almonds in the pools underfoot. Every drip is amplified in the close confines of the drift, and every scar in the rock face a testimony to the extraordinary endeavours of the men who worked the mine. Scattered about the site are the abandoned remains of the sorting floors, the washing pools and smelting furnaces, great conical lumps of slag, old broken rusty buckets, all somehow incongruous in this pastoral setting.

These are the kind of hills that roll away into the distance in every direction. You climb to the top of a hill only to find there is another top beyond, and many more tops again. On a clear day the hills stretch away as far as you can see in fifty shades of indigo. Deep sykes of sparkling water with mystical names cascade down the hillsides. Miles of centuries-old drystone dykes, decorated with a lacework of silver and orange lichens and bright green mosses, provide shelter from the harsh upland winds, and nesting sites for the wheatears and whinchats on their return home from Africa to raise their young. In spring the coarse brown tussocks of wiry grass give way to myriad delicate wild flowers, the hill studded with bright jewels of purple and pink and yellow – speedwells, tormentils, milkwort, lousewort, butterwort, orchids and violets, and rare bog and heath plants – all with their place in medicinal folklore and all coexisting happily with the grazing native sheep.

I come here to watch the changing seasons, to feel the wind in my hair and the rain on my face. I come when the snow has filled the hollows and coated the dykes with icing. I come to see the old bent hawthorn and the solitary rowan tree with its roots thrust determinedly between two rocks and to catch the haunting cry of the curlew in spring, or a glimpse of the noble mountain hare in the half light of winter. I come to gather the canny and self-reliant sheep into the enclosures, my faithful collie at my side.

And at the end of the day I return to the farm, past the stone barn where the ancient stall for the horse stands empty, the hay heck draped in cobwebs, past the grain store where oatmeal was put for winter keep for the mining community, and past the old slate-roofed schoolhouse built back in 1794 for the miners' children, and back to my home and my kitchen and my desk, to today's faster moving world of smart technology, cyberculture and electronic communications, safe in the knowledge that there is another place – my favourite place – out there in the hills, where time almost stands still. ■

Talk of Armadale Trees

Susan Anwin

QUIET. SUNSHINE. The scent of resin in the air. None of which excited the ant. It carried the crumb to the colony, not minding the girl who stopped in the pine grove to contemplate the canopy and to soak up the environment.

She stayed just for a couple of days in Armadale on the Isle of Skye and chanced upon this pine grove during one of her daytrips. The girl didn't know it yet, but this would end up as her sharpest memory of the Scotland roundtrip, clearer than the standing stones of Orkney, clearer than the black sand on the lonely beach, parting in the wake of her stick as she etched the names of her imaginary friends into it.

She never noticed the ant as she listened to the soft conversation of the trees, one occasional crack at a time and the rustle of the wind among the pine-needles.

The ant didn't take note of her either. It just carried the crumb on in the sunlit silence. ∎

Little Fields

Ailat Murnau

Under the lead sky, the lead hills
A curlew on a stone, and a five o' clock curfew
We tread carefully, as on a minefield
This place is sacred, damned, magnificent

Little Sparta is the finer opulence of simplicity
Professor Dutton cherished in his poetry
he's dead now
and so's Finlay

What will become of this land?
A place that heard
the private anger of a wordsmith

Stony paths lead to Little Spartas

Little fields long for horizons...

■

Kettins Village

Alex Nicoll

MY FAVOURITE place in Scotland is Kettins village. Kettins? You've never heard of it? I'm not surprised, neither have most other people. Where is it? you say. I'm almost frightened to tell you in case it gets spoiled by incoming hordes with big cars, beer cans and litter! Well, it's about a mile from Coupar Angus, a short distance from the Coupar Angus – Dundee road. It could almost be a location for a remake of Brigadoon with its scattering of cottages, babbling burn, church and school. Nearby too is the estate of Hallyburton, once the home of the Laird of Pitcur. He was a strong supporter of Bonnie Dundee, and was killed at the Battle of Killiecrankie in 1689. (He's mentioned in Burns' poem about Killiecrankie.)

On 28th November 1934, three weeks before my eighth birthday, I move with my family to Pitcur Farm, two and a quarter miles from Coupar Angus, also just off the Coupar Angus – Dundee road. I remember the date well as the next day, 29th November was a public holiday to celebrate the wedding of Princess Marina of Greece to the Duke of Kent. Thus is it was the following Monday 3rd December I had my first visit to Kettins village when I went there to the local country school of three classrooms, a work area for woodwork, science and girls' domestic. There were three female teachers, single ladies dedicated to education. One of them was the daughter of the local postman. The headmaster was a wee old-time Scottish Dominie whose interests were Botany and Astronomy. He had an observatory built in the school garden and took the pupils out to study the stars and planets in the early winter evenings. The ethos of the school was simple; hard work and more hard work. Such was the quality of the education there that when, in 1939, I won a bursary and went to a secondary school in Blairgowrie I was a year ahead of the class in algebra and geometry.

Three weeks after we first started there, in December 1934, we attended the school Christmas party. It was an unforgettable day for me as it was the first time I had ever seen a Christmas tree. Christmas was not even a public holiday in Scotland in the early thirties. New Year was still the big thing.

Encouraged by my parents, I sometimes went to Sunday School in the village church, the interior of which is a place of beauty and peace, all stained glass windows and plush seating. Outside the rear door of the church is a concrete erection on which is mounted a historical bell brought all the way from Holland in the early seventeenth century. Near the burn is the old village pump. It is still working if you know how to fang it with water from the burn.

In November 1939 our family moved away from the area when my father found employment near Meigle. The Dominie at Kettins did not forget us however and wrote a very sympathetic letter to our mother when one of my sisters lost her life in a tragic drowning accident in 1941.

In 1948 my parents retired to a house in Coupar Angus and once again Kettins village became an important place for me. Helen, the girl who was to become my wife, had settled in the village and she was employed in the local printing firm in Coupar Angus. She was an attractive, blonde, Highland lassie with a soft Inverness accent and many of the local young men admired her. I was one of them, and when I attended her firm's annual dance I quickly made her acquaintance. We danced together most of the night and I walked with her to her home in Kettins.

In July 1954 we were married in the lovely village church, and moved straight away to a house in Dundee where I was working. We made regular visits to the village of course while her parents were there. They eventually moved to Dundee as well in the sixties.

My wife was very domesticated and her home baking was in constant demand by our church, friends and neighbours. Her greatest love, however, was flowers, gardening and all nature. Our house was home to a sundry of rescued cats and dogs.

With her round unwrinkled face, and her blonde hair, Helen looked much younger than her years and people wondered why she had a bus pass. She was always neatly dressed, used discreet make up and had a gentle smiling manner. I was proud to be seen with her.

The house we came to when we were married in 1954 is the only home we ever had, and I'm still living in it. Sad to say, however, my wife passed away in March this year and I now share the house with a cat called Henry, and a dog called Pippa, both animals rescued by my wife. Fortunately for me, our two daughters have homes nearby and they give me incredible and unselfish support. This enables me to carry on and do the best I can. Many times, especially when I'm alone at night, my thoughts return to Kettins village. It is the place where I received my formative education and where I met my lovely wife. Yes, it will always be my special place. My favourite place. ∎

Bella's Kitchen

Simone Sinclair

MY FAVOURITE place is Bella's kitchen. It was always safe and warm in my Granny Bella's 'wee hoose' in Cleeves Road, Nitshill, Glasgow. After a short run across the city on the dirty number 10 bus, with my headphones on, I would get off and walk through the scheme to Granny's.

'There ye are hen, come in and lock that door behind ye.'

Once inside I always felt at home. Everything in Granny's house was familiar and comforting: the smell of home-made Scotch broth steaming from the gas stove; the old-fashioned multi-coloured bottles and potions in her bathroom; the white candlewick bedspread and dark crucifix in her bedroom; and the tea set-filled glass cabinet in her sitting room. As a wee girl I loved to look through the glass at the fragile china, which was delicately painted with exotic birds and flowers.

I remember when I took Al there to meet her for the first time.

'Does that boy want soup?' she shouted at me over the too-loud telly. She was too shy to ask him herself. She served him his soup first, before we got ours. Poor Al sat, alone and confused, at the Dettol-scrubbed kitchen table, while the 'wimmin' sat in the sitting room next door and ate from our laps. She'd set out his plate and a newspaper for him to read while he ate. I stifled a giggle as I heard Al's spoon clattering against his plate. I knew he was wondering why he was eating alone. Mum laughed while she explained later, that this was just 'Granny's way'.

'She's old school. She used to serve my daddy his dinner that way.'

Granny was old school all right! She used to say things like, 'Tell the truth and shame the devil' and 'God bless us and save us', while crossing herself. But I only knew her as my Granny.

My plump Granny: she made homemade soup and roast chicken and mashed potatoes. My fun Granny: she loved the bingo and took me on holiday to Blackpool. My wise Granny: she taught me to tell the time and tie my shoelaces. My beautiful Granny: her steely grey hair was always perfectly coiffed, set with a mist of hairspray, and protected beneath a silky head-scarf. My patient Granny: she serenely sat and read the paper while we kids ran wild. 'Calm down, you'll make yourselves sick. Watch now!' (All said without missing a single word on the page.)

My houseproud Granny: her home was always spot-less and warm with the coal fire roaring. My clever Granny: she loved a good whodunnit. (Agatha Christie, Taggart and Columbo were her favourites.) My Granny, 'Oor wee Bella': she solved murders alongside Hercule Poirot and Miss Marple all night. She could never sleep through the night after spending years cleaning buses on the nightshift.

Of course Bella wasn't just my Granny, and wasn't just my 'mammy's mammy'. She'd had her own life too. Although I only caught a tiny glimpse of this 'other' life, I know it had its fair share of hard times and loss.

Bella Riley: she'd had seven children. Only five

survived, including the youngest, my mum. Bella Riley: her old house was bombed in the war years ago. A direct hit cracked right through the roof and then the ceiling, but not one dish on her Welsh dresser had been smashed. Isabella Riley, neé Wilson: she'd married my dapper jack-the-lad granddad at sixteen. Bella Wilson: she'd worked as a housemaid at a grand house in London when she was only young. The proud lady of the house insisted on calling her Isa (Bella was too common a name for service you see). But Bella had missed her 'mammy' and come home again to Glasgow.

Wee Bella Wilson: she'd lost her beloved 'mammy and daddy' young, and so she helped bring up her five little sisters. Wee Bella Wilson: she was born in 1918 and had seen poor folk starving during the depression. These early experiences of poverty made her a lifelong socialist with a passion for fairness. Bella Wilson: she didn't care much for school but made sure we all did well. Bella: her usually placid mum had slapped the teacher, after the teacher walloped wee Bella in class. Great-Gran had seen red, marched up to the school and slapped the auld harridan so hard that her wig fell off.

'All the weans clapped and cheered,' Bella remembered later, tears of laughter in her eyes.

So, Bella wasn't just my Granny, and wasn't just my 'mammy's mammy'. She'd had this whole other life before any of us existed, in a world totally unrecognisable to us. She worked and strived to bring up her family and to clothe and feed and nurture them, and us, with all her power. Life's hardships didn't dull her lust for life or make her bitter. She was always the kindest soul with seemingly endless love and patience. Even at the end, she showed no fear, and her face was a picture of peace as she passed away.

Every day her unwavering, fierce and strong love still warms me. Every day I hear her words:

'Look after yer mammy darlin'.'

'I will Bella,' I always answer.

Someone else lives in that house now. It's probably another wee 'wumman'. Maybe she's someone else's Granny. But Bella's Kitchen always remains the same, and is suspended unchanged in my mind. Bella's Kitchen will always be safe and warm and welcoming. Bella's Kitchen will always be my favourite place and Bella will always be there waiting for me.

'There ye are hen, come in.' ∎

My Favourite Place is the outcome of a project run by Scottish Book Trust, in partnership with BBC Radio Scotland, throughout 2012. People from all over the country were invited to write stories, poems, lyrics, letters and diary entries about their favourite place in Scotland. This book contains a selection of the best of these, as well as some special pieces by authors and leading Scottish artists.

This book is available in e-book, large print and full audio versions, all free to download. For more details, please visit **www.scottishbooktrust.com/myfavouriteplace/thebook**.

To read all of the submissions to the My Favourite Place project and browse our story map of Scotland, please visit **www.scottishbooktrust.com/myfavouriteplace**.